THE LITTLE BOOK OF

LIGHT

CODES

JOURNAL

LAARA

ISBN: 978-1950367214

Published by
Lifestyle Entrepreneurs Press
Las Vegas, NV

If you are interested in publishing through Lifestyle Entrepreneurs Press, write to Publishing@LifestyleEntrepreneursPress.com

Publications or foreign rights acquisitions of our catalog books.
Learn More: www.LifestyleEntrepreneursPress.com

Printed in the USA

Welcome to Your *Little Book of Light Codes* Personal Journal

This journal is part of the companion support material for *The Little Book of Light Codes*, and can be used alongside the book and Oracle deck. In the journal, you will find renderings of all fifty-two symbols, followed by empty pages in which to write about your unique process with each symbol. As you navigate through the book, we encourage you to write about your inspirations and insights. It can be helpful and fun to look back and realize how far you've come!

Journaling provides far more than a valuable record of your life experience. Journaling provides you with an opportunity and a tool to help you work through confusion in search of clarity. Your journal provides a safe space in which you can express your innermost thoughts and feelings; it gives you permission to articulate emotions and energies which otherwise might be difficult to process. It can also help you to connect with Spirit in profound ways, whether it be with levels of your own soul, or with the Beings of Love and Light who support you unconditionally on your path through life.

As you work with your journal, please know that you are supported by the healing energies of Lady Isis and Jeshua. We all wish you blessings of Love for your amazing and wonderful journey. May you heal swiftly with ease and grace, and find clarity as the Love that you are.

With Love,
—*Laara*

Lakahana

(Lah-kah-ha-nah)

Embody Love and Harmony, Trust Yourself and Others, Release Fear

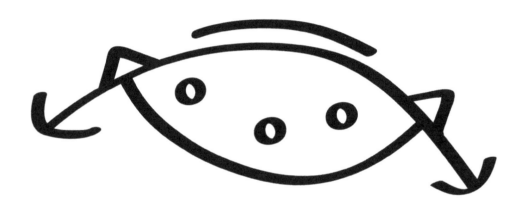

Gamma

(Gam-mah)

Opening Channels of Light, Connecting to Source, Breaking Through, Dissolving Barriers

Yah'kma

(Yah-k-mah, with a break before the 'k')

Creating a Sacred Healing Space

_____

_____

_____

_____

_____

_____

_____

_____

_____

_____

_____

_____

Akahanama

(Ah-kah-ha-nah-mah)

Freedom to Choose, Freedom to Release, Freedom to Be the Love that You Are

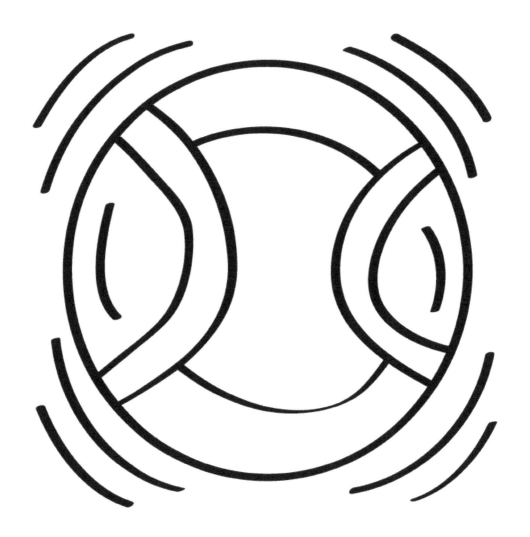

Yah'tkh

(Yaa-tuck)

"Just Be" — Being Centered and Grounded with Integrity and Inner Strength

Rugth

(Roo-g-th)

Being Centered and Grounded, Gently
Maintaining Respectful Boundaries

Scryb'th

(Scrib-th)

Warming the Heart, Supporting a Healthy Path, Expanding Self

Ahagma

(Ah-ha-g-mah)

Integrating, Taking the Next Step,
Relasing Resistance, Making Progress

Kh'mak

(K'mac)

Time, Presence, Flow, Freedom Breath

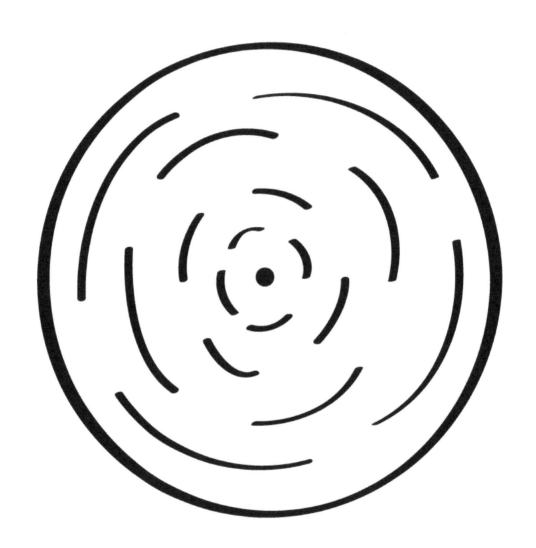

Turla

(Tour-la)

Stillpoint

Tsuhami

(Tsu-ha-mi)

Butterlfy Wings: Spread Your Wings and Fly, Release Resistance, Trust

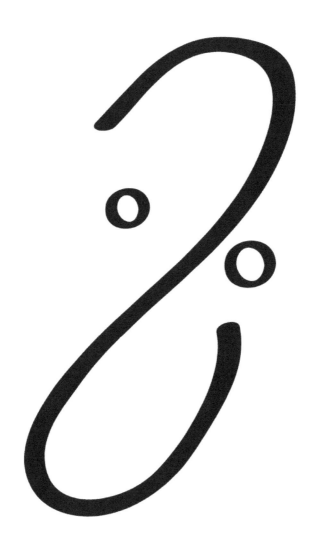

Turmar

(Toor-mar)

Unity

Teglih

(Teg-li)

Healing the Physical Plane (Mother Earth, Her Plants, and the Physical Body)

Kahlsi

(Kel-si)

Respect, Honor, Love, Gratitude

Hydahama

(Hi-da-hahma)

Openness, Living in Harmony, Flow

Bahan

(Ba-han)

Forgiveness

Halahma

(Hala-hma)

Finding Inner Fire, Strength, and Clarity
(Useful for Healing Abuse or Abuse of Substances, and for Addiction Recovery)

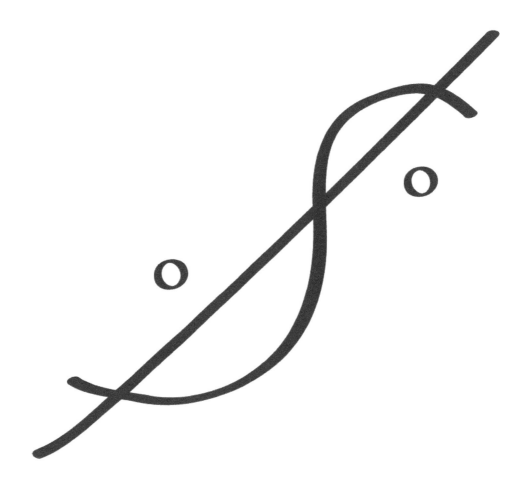

Khalagma

(Ka-lag-ma)

Releasing Mis-Qualified Energies,
Removing Obstacles

Hoitma

(Hoy-t-ma)

Cleansing Breath, Clearing Lungs

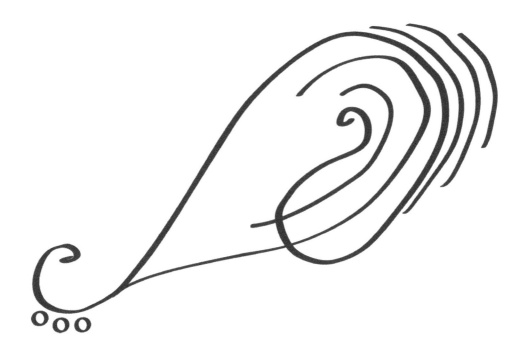

Dahanama

(Da-ha-na-ma)

Release Pain in the Physical Body

Go to Beauty and Peace

Go to Beauty and Peace

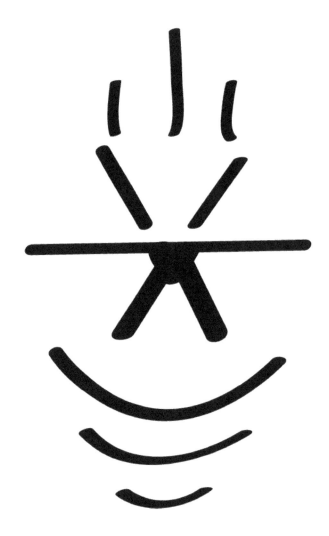

Pahma

(Pah-ma)

Love of the Highest Order

Lahma

(La-chh-ma - softly)

Non-Attachment, Letting Go, Freedom

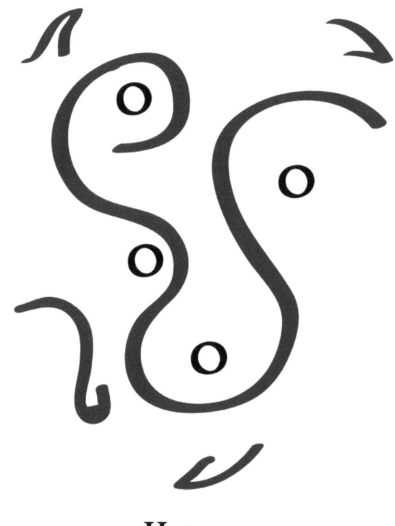

Henama

(He-na-ma)

Healing Sexual Abuse and Trauma

_____

_____

_____

_____

_____

_____

_____

_____

_____

_____

_____

Aman'kh

(A-monk)

Expression, Trust, Surrender, Freedom,
Embrace Your Path

Jamaka

(Ja-ma-ka)

Centering, Moving through Overwhelm, Taking One Step at a Time

Akuna

(A-ku-na)

Trusting Your Experience, Belonging

Yunami

(Yu-na-mi)

Remember, Reflect, Gain Clarity, Make Connections

Humbelah

(Hum-bel-ah)

Heart Full of Gratitude

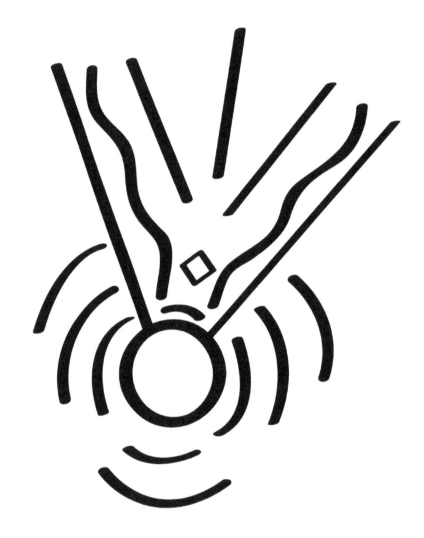

Delight

Seeing Clearly, No Confusion:
Remembering Who We Are

Kahalula

(Ka-ha-lu-la)

The Love Felt Between Twin Souls

Pahgyahma

(Pah-gyah-ma)

Healing with Earth and Sun Energy

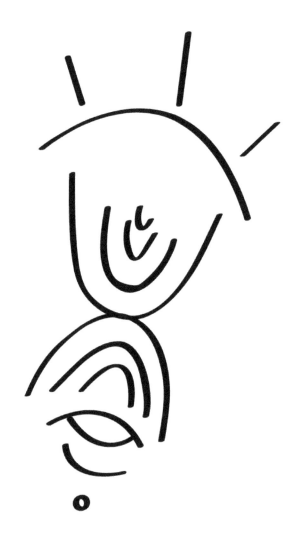

Yahma

(Yah-ma)

Transfer of Energy

Hennami

(Hen-naa-mi)

Higher Communication, Connecting with Spirit/Beings, Being Protected by Light and the Highest Integrity

Gyla

(Gai-la)

Coming to Fruition, Growth, Expansion, Development, Cretion, and Creativity

Kahli

(Kah-li)

Karma

Ughma

(Ugg-ma)

Connection to Soul, Soul Retrieval, Authentic Self

Suri

(Tsu-ri)

Enlightenment

Commagt

(Com-ma-gt)

Releasing Confusion

Zahay'kma

(Za-hay-kma)

Forgiving Self

Anami

(A-na-mi)

Finding and Developing Self-Love

The Love That You Are

Self-Love, Knowing One's Worth, Expression of Self

Jyak'ma

(Yak-ma)

Self-Reflection, Self-Discovery, Self-Exploration

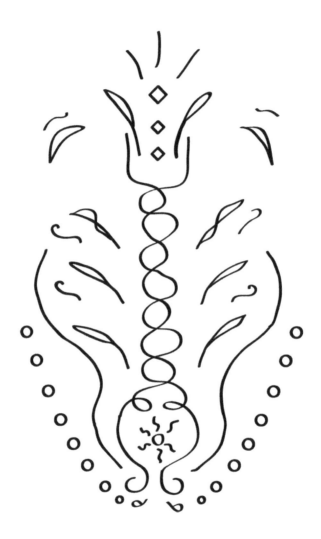

Galagma

(Ga-laa-g-ma)

Love from Within, Kundalini Energy

Tungah

(Tung-ah)

Aligning with Information

Kalak'tuk

(Ka-lak-tuk)

Integrating Dimensions, Moving through Dimensions, Collapsing Time

Lakama

(La-ka-ma)

Turn Outward Beauty into Inner Beauty

Shizama

(Shi-za-ma)

Releasing Negative Energy Space

Jayagk

(Jai-yack)

Release Toxins on All Levels

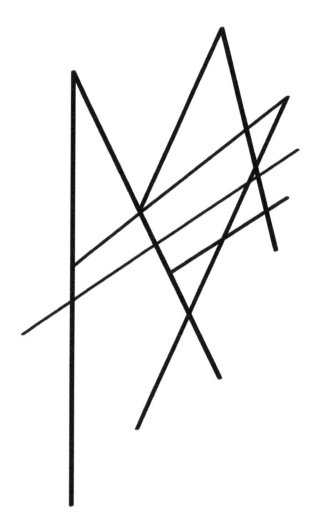

Panma

(Pan-ma)

Moving with Light, Expanding Frequencies

Kalimar

(Kal-i-mar)

Divine Unity, Soul Family

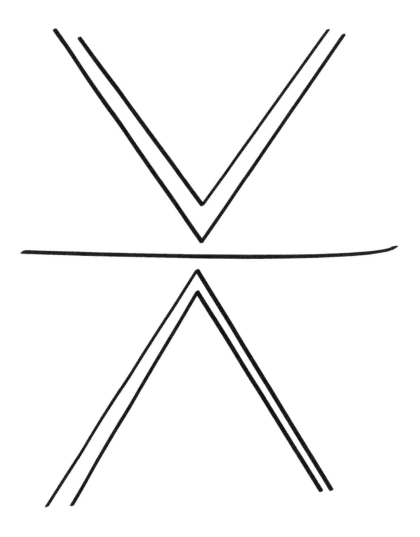

I AM Presence

I am the Consciousness of I AM

CPSIA information can be obtained
at www.ICGtesting.com
Printed in the USA
LVHW060109231120
672437LV00031B/364